WELCOME TO THE U.S.A.
MINNESOTA

Written by Ann Heinrichs   Illustrated by Matt Kania
Content Advisers: Doug Anderson, Community and Private Forest
Supervisor, Minnesota Department of Natural Resources,
Saint Paul, Minnesota, and Jean Anderson,
Historian, Forest Lake, Minnesota

The Child's World

Published in the United States of America by The Child's World®
PO Box 326 • Chanhassen, MN 55317-0326
800-599-READ • www.childsworld.com

Photo Credits

Cover: Don Enger/Animals Animals/Earth Scenes; frontispiece: Photodisc.

Interior: AP/Wide World Photos: 21 (Brainerd Daily Dispatch), 30 (Jim Mone); Getty Images/Stone/Paul Chesley: 29; Mark E. Gibson/Corbis: 33; Great Lakes Floating Maritime Museum: 22; Hormel: 34; Layne Kennedy/Corbis: 9, 14; Minnesota Historical Society: 17 (Ann Olson Bercher/Oliver H. Kelly Farm), 18; David Muench/Corbis: 6, 13; North Star Publishing: 10; John A. Peterson/Scandinavian Hjemkomst Festival: 25; Michael Portner: 26.

Acknowledgments

The Child's World®: Mary Berendes, Publishing Director

Editorial Directions, Inc.: E. Russell Primm, Editorial Director; Katie Marsico, Associate Editor; Judith Shiffer, Assistant Editor; Matt Messbarger, Editorial Assistant; Susan Hindman, Copy Editor; Melissa McDaniel, Proofreader; Kevin Cunningham, Peter Garnham, Matt Messbarger, Olivia Nellums, Chris Simms, Molly Symmonds, Katherine Trickle, Carl Stephen Wender, Fact Checkers; Tim Griffin/IndexServ, Indexer; Cian Loughlin O'Day, Photo Researcher and Editor

The Design Lab: Kathleen Petelinsek, Design; Julia Goozen, Art Production

Library of Congress Cataloging-in-Publication Data

Heinrichs, Ann.
  Minnesota / by Ann Heinrichs ; cartography and illustrations by Matt Kania.
    p. cm. — (Welcome to the U.S.A.)
  Includes index.
  ISBN 1-59296-474-5 (library bound : alk. paper)
  1. Minnesota—Juvenile literature. I. Kania, Matt, ill. II. Title. II. Series.
  F606.3.H453 2006
  977.6—dc22   2005008873

Ann Heinrichs is the author of more than 100 books for children and young adults. She has also enjoyed successful careers as a children's book editor and an advertising copywriter. Ann grew up in Fort Smith, Arkansas, and lives in Chicago, Illinois.

**About the Author
Ann Heinrichs**

Matt Kania loves maps and, as a kid, dreamed of making them. In school he studied geography and cartography, and today he makes maps for a living. Matt's favorite thing about drawing maps is learning about the places they represent. Many of the maps he has created can be found in books, magazines, videos, Web sites, and public places.

**About the
Map Illustrator
Matt Kania**

On the cover: A mother loon and her chicks float along on a Minnesota lake.
On page one: It's hard to miss the skyline of Minneapolis, Minnesota's largest city.

OUR MINNESOTA TRIP

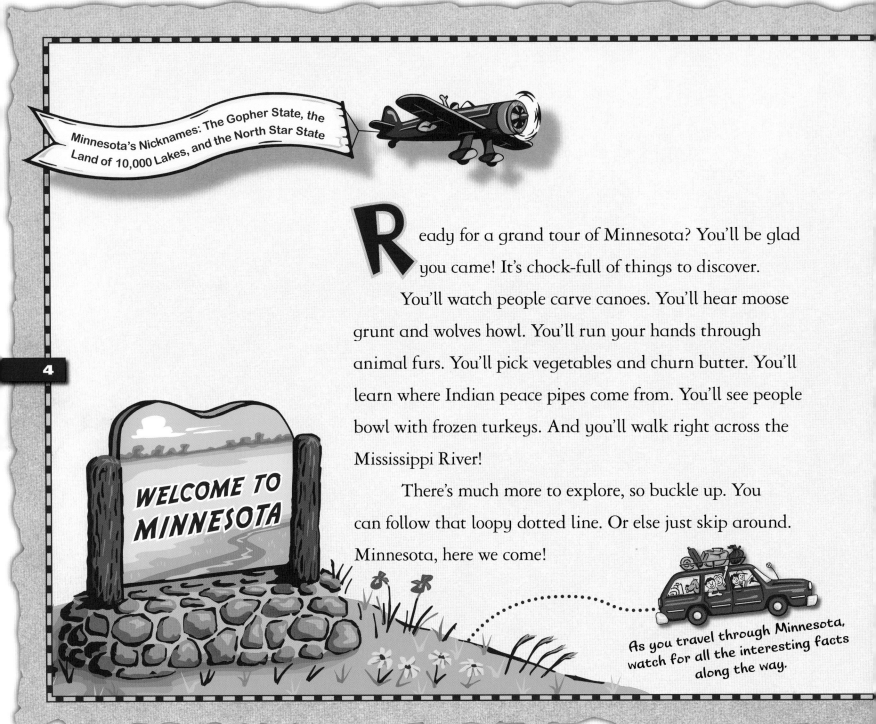

Minnesota's Nicknames: The Gopher State, the Land of 10,000 Lakes, and the North Star State

WELCOME TO MINNESOTA

Ready for a grand tour of Minnesota? You'll be glad you came! It's chock-full of things to discover.

You'll watch people carve canoes. You'll hear moose grunt and wolves howl. You'll run your hands through animal furs. You'll pick vegetables and churn butter. You'll learn where Indian peace pipes come from. You'll see people bowl with frozen turkeys. And you'll walk right across the Mississippi River!

There's much more to explore, so buckle up. You can follow that loopy dotted line. Or else just skip around. Minnesota, here we come!

As you travel through Minnesota, watch for all the interesting facts along the way.

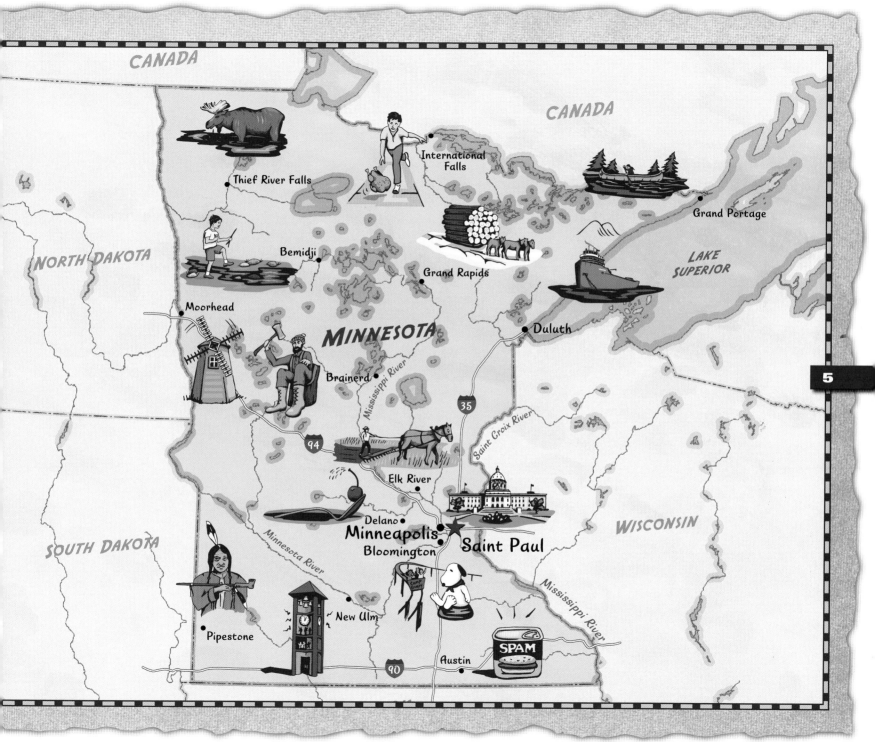

CANADA

CANADA

NORTH DAKOTA

Thief River Falls

International Falls

Grand Portage

Bemidji

LAKE SUPERIOR

Moorhead

Grand Rapids

MINNESOTA

Duluth

Brainerd

Mississippi River

Saint Croix River

94

35

Elk River

Delano

WISCONSIN

Minneapolis

Saint Paul

Minnesota River

Bloomington

SOUTH DAKOTA

Pipestone

New Ulm

Mississippi River

Austin

SPAM

90

Want a peek at the source of the Mississippi?
Take a trip to Lake Itasca!

Minnesota actually has 12,034 lakes that are larger than 10 acres (4 ha).

Want to cross the Mississippi River? You can do it on foot! Just go to Lake Itasca, near Bemidji. It's the source of the Mississippi River. You can wade across the river where it begins. Or leap across on stepping-stones. Just watch out! Those rocks are slippery!

Minnesota is called the Land of 10,000 Lakes. Lake Itasca is just one of them. Lake Superior borders northeastern Minnesota. It's one of the nation's five Great Lakes.

Northern Minnesota is rough and rugged. The state's highest points are in this region. The rest of Minnesota is mostly rolling plains. They make rich farmland.

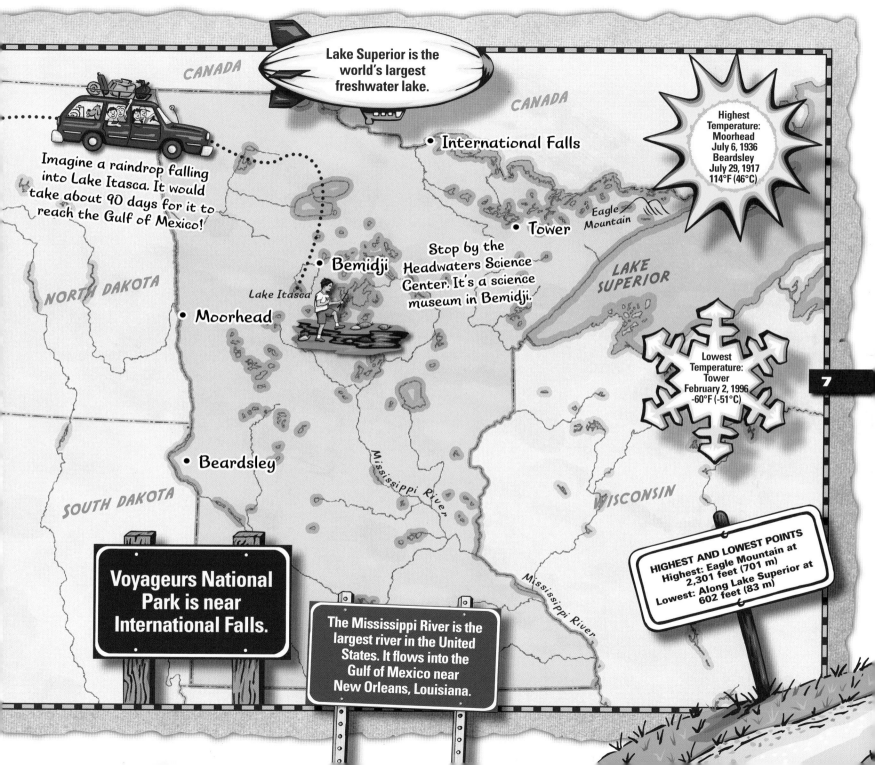

Lake Superior is the world's largest freshwater lake.

CANADA

CANADA

International Falls

Imagine a raindrop falling into Lake Itasca. It would take about 90 days for it to reach the Gulf of Mexico!

Tower

Eagle Mountain

Highest Temperature: Moorhead July 6, 1936 Beardsley July 29, 1917 114°F (46°C)

Bemidji

Stop by the Headwaters Science Center. It's a science museum in Bemidji.

NORTH DAKOTA

Lake Itasca

LAKE SUPERIOR

Moorhead

Lowest Temperature: Tower February 2, 1996 -60°F (-51°C)

Beardsley

Mississippi River

SOUTH DAKOTA

WISCONSIN

Mississippi River

Voyageurs National Park is near International Falls.

The Mississippi River is the largest river in the United States. It flows into the Gulf of Mexico near New Orleans, Louisiana.

HIGHEST AND LOWEST POINTS
Highest: Eagle Mountain at 2,301 feet (701 m)
Lowest: Along Lake Superior at 602 feet (83 m)

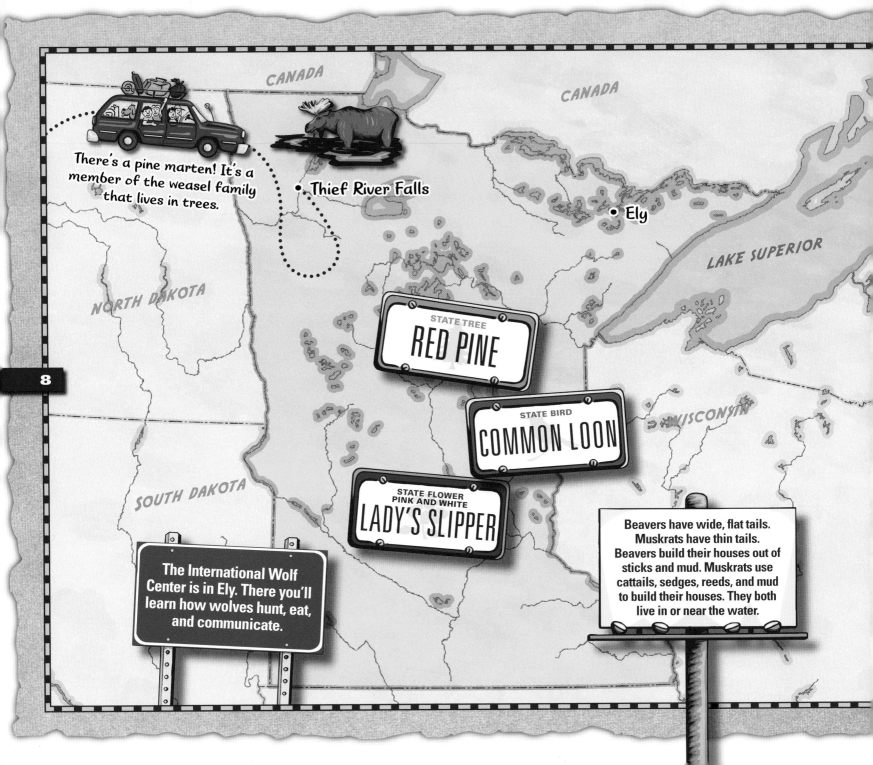

CANADA

CANADA

There's a pine marten! It's a member of the weasel family that lives in trees.

• Thief River Falls

• Ely

NORTH DAKOTA

LAKE SUPERIOR

8

STATE TREE
RED PINE

STATE BIRD
COMMON LOON

WISCONSIN

SOUTH DAKOTA

STATE FLOWER
PINK AND WHITE
LADY'S SLIPPER

Beavers have wide, flat tails. Muskrats have thin tails. Beavers build their houses out of sticks and mud. Muskrats use cattails, sedges, reeds, and mud to build their houses. They both live in or near the water.

The International Wolf Center is in Ely. There you'll learn how wolves hunt, eat, and communicate.

Agassiz National Wildlife Refuge

Do you hear a deep grunt or whine? It could be a moose! Do you hear howling? It could be a coyote or a wolf! Do you hear a crazy yodeling call? It could be a waterbird called a loon!

You're roaming through Agassiz National Wildlife Refuge. It's in northwestern Minnesota, near Thief River Falls.

Minnesota's forests are full of wildlife. You'll see big deer and little foxes. You'll glimpse sleek minks and otters. Fat woodchucks and muskrats waddle along. And giant Canada geese drift across the lakes. Just creep quietly and perk up your ears!

This timber wolf calls Minnesota's forests home.

The National Park Service has 5 sites in Minnesota.

Icebox Days in International Falls

Strike! Try turkey bowling in International Falls!

Do you like winter sports? Then you'll love Icebox Days. It's a crazy festival of winter sports. You can try "smoosh" racing through the snow. Big boards are strapped to your feet. Or you might like turkey bowling. You'll use frozen turkeys instead of bowling balls!

Minnesota's a great place for winter fun. People enjoy skiing, sledding, snowmobiling, and ice-skating. Hockey is a popular team sport, too.

In warm weather, people head for the lakes. They go swimming, waterskiing, and fishing. The forests are great for hiking and camping. You'll enjoy Minnesota any time of the year!

Do you watch *Rocky and Bullwinkle* cartoons? This flying squirrel and moose say their hometown is Frostbite Falls. It's based on International Falls!

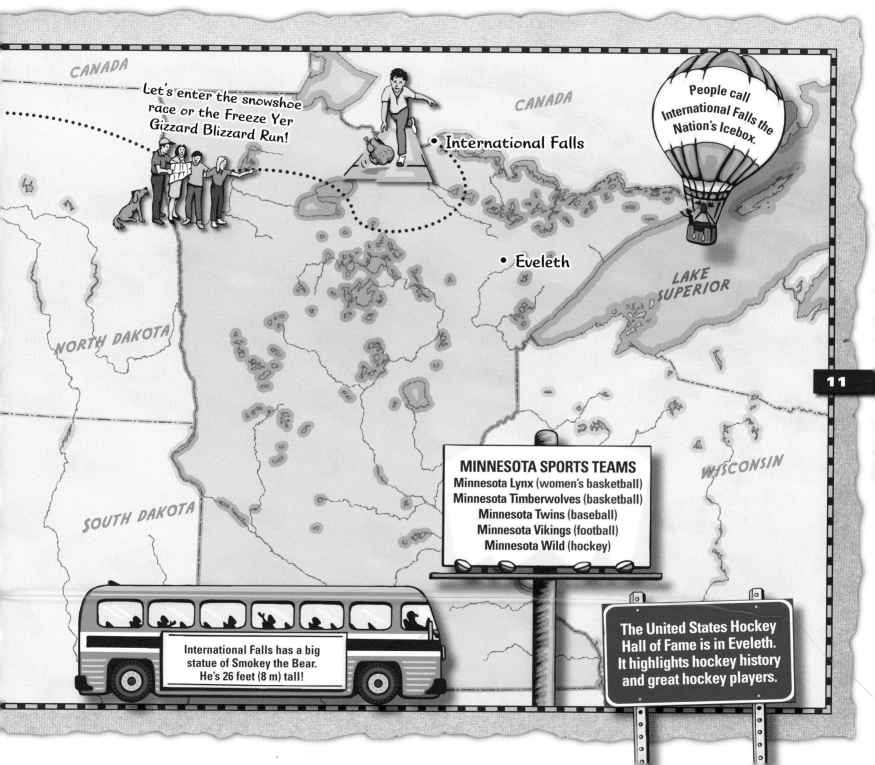

CANADA

Let's enter the snowshoe race or the Freeze Yer Gizzard Blizzard Run!

CANADA

• International Falls

People call International Falls the Nation's Icebox.

• Eveleth

LAKE SUPERIOR

NORTH DAKOTA

SOUTH DAKOTA

WISCONSIN

MINNESOTA SPORTS TEAMS
Minnesota Lynx (women's basketball)
Minnesota Timberwolves (basketball)
Minnesota Twins (baseball)
Minnesota Vikings (football)
Minnesota Wild (hockey)

International Falls has a big statue of Smokey the Bear. He's 26 feet (8 m) tall!

The United States Hockey Hall of Fame is in Eveleth. It highlights hockey history and great hockey players.

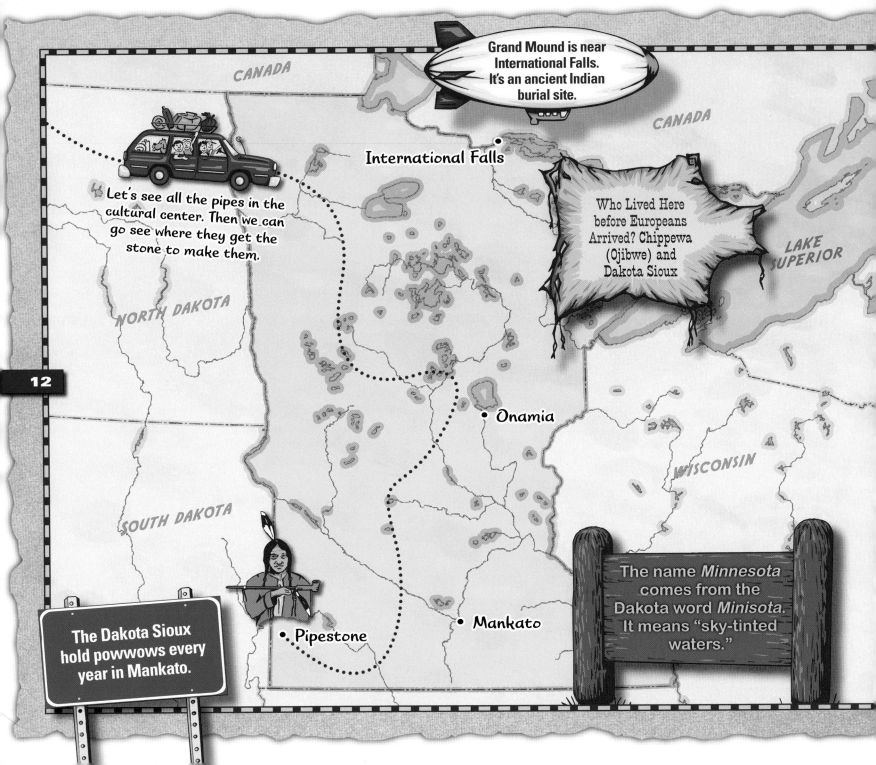

Grand Mound is near International Falls. It's an ancient Indian burial site.

CANADA

CANADA

International Falls

Let's see all the pipes in the cultural center. Then we can go see where they get the stone to make them.

Who Lived Here before Europeans Arrived? Chippewa (Ojibwe) and Dakota Sioux

LAKE SUPERIOR

NORTH DAKOTA

Onamia

SOUTH DAKOTA

WISCONSIN

The Dakota Sioux hold powwows every year in Mankato.

Pipestone

Mankato

The name *Minnesota* comes from the Dakota word *Minisota*. It means "sky-tinted waters."

Pipestone National Monument

Feel the rough, red pipestone. It's soft and easy to carve. You're visiting Pipestone National Monument. It's in the town of Pipestone. You can watch a carving demonstration here. You'll learn how to carve and drill the stone.

Native Americans once traveled here from far away. They collected the stone for carving peace pipes. American Indians still collect pipestone here today.

Thousands of Dakota Sioux once lived in Minnesota. They built rounded homes with branches and hides. They hunted forest animals for food. The Ojibwe, or Chippewa, arrived in the late 1600s. They came from Wisconsin, to the east.

Want to learn how Native Americans carved peace pipes? Just visit Pipestone National Monument.

Mille Lacs Indian Museum is in Onamia.

Have you traveled back in time? No, you're just visiting Grand Portage National Monument!

Medard Chouart, Sieur des Groseilliers, and Pierre Esprit Radisson were Minnesota's 1st white explorers.

Fur Trading at Grand Portage

R un your hands through thick animal furs. Smell the freshly baked bread. See the canoes built by hand. You're visiting Grand Portage National Monument! It brings Minnesota's fur-trading days to life.

French fur traders arrived in about 1660. They were the first white people in Minnesota. Several fur companies soon moved in. They hired French-Canadian **voyageurs.** The voyageurs traveled by canoe and on foot. They went between trading posts and the wilderness.

Grand Portage was an important trading post. Voyageurs and the Ojibwe met and traded there. Every summer, they all gathered for a **rendezvous.** They exchanged goods, food, stories, and games.

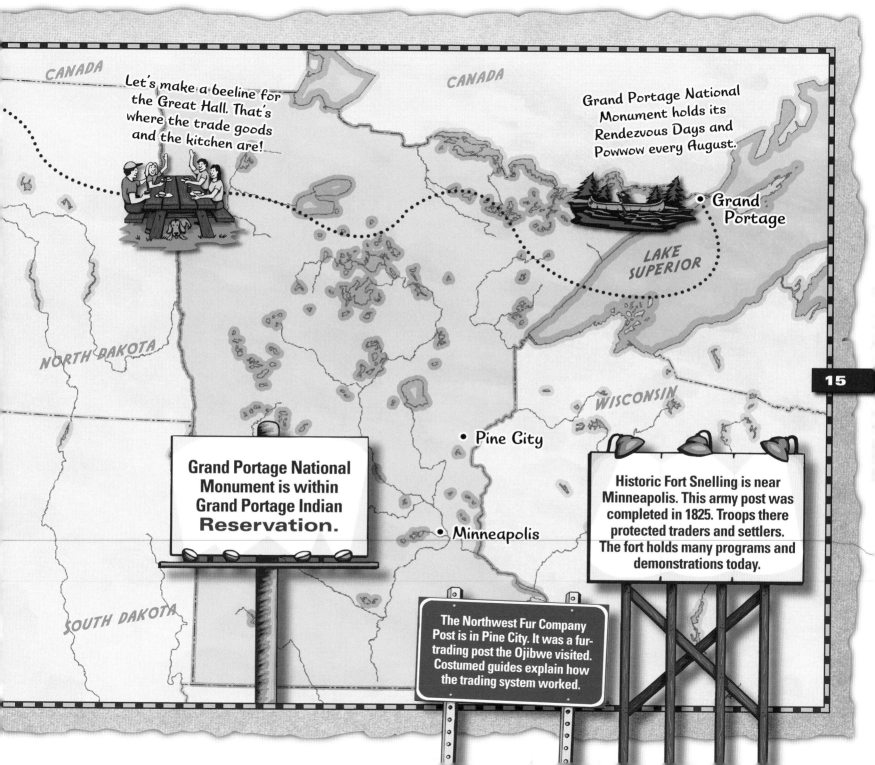

Let's make a beeline for the Great Hall. That's where the trade goods and the kitchen are!

Grand Portage National Monument holds its Rendezvous Days and Powwow every August.

CANADA

CANADA

• Grand Portage

LAKE SUPERIOR

NORTH DAKOTA

WISCONSIN

• Pine City

SOUTH DAKOTA

• Minneapolis

Grand Portage National Monument is within Grand Portage Indian Reservation.

Historic Fort Snelling is near Minneapolis. This army post was completed in 1825. Troops there protected traders and settlers. The fort holds many programs and demonstrations today.

The Northwest Fur Company Post is in Pine City. It was a fur-trading post the Ojibwe visited. Costumed guides explain how the trading system worked.

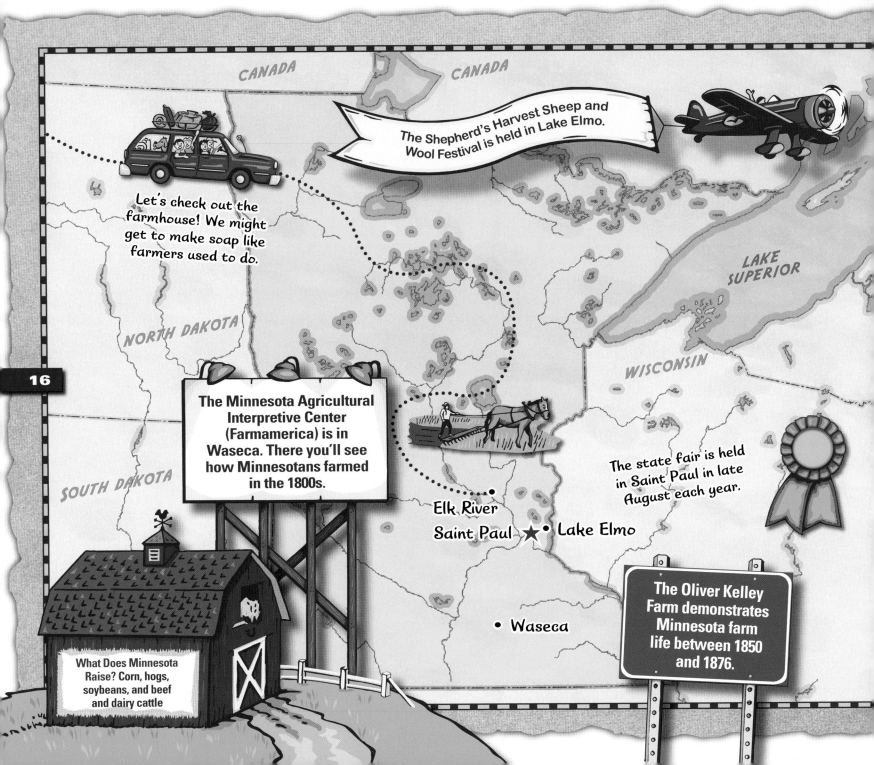

CANADA

CANADA

The Shepherd's Harvest Sheep and Wool Festival is held in Lake Elmo.

Let's check out the farmhouse! We might get to make soap like farmers used to do.

LAKE SUPERIOR

16

NORTH DAKOTA

WISCONSIN

The Minnesota Agricultural Interpretive Center (Farmamerica) is in Waseca. There you'll see how Minnesotans farmed in the 1800s.

SOUTH DAKOTA

The state fair is held in Saint Paul in late August each year.

Elk River
Saint Paul ★ • Lake Elmo

• Waseca

The Oliver Kelley Farm demonstrates Minnesota farm life between 1850 and 1876.

What Does Minnesota Raise? Corn, hogs, soybeans, and beef and dairy cattle

Elk River's Oliver Kelley Farm

Animals roam inside the barn. Farmworkers plough fields using oxen and horses. Fresh vegetables are growing in the garden. You're visiting the Oliver Kelley Farm!

This is a living history farm. It shows how farmers lived in the 1800s. The farmworkers all wear 1860s clothing. And they explain just what they're doing.

Farming has always been important in Minnesota. Today, farms cover more than half the state. Hogs are the most valuable farm animals. Beef and dairy cattle are important, too. Corn and soybeans are the leading crops. They make great meals for farm animals!

Want to explore the Oliver Kelley Farm? Just hop on a hayride!

Minnesota ranks among the top 10 states in corn, soybeans, hogs, dairy cows, and cheese production.

Would you make a good lumberjack? Tour Grand Rapids' Forest History Center and find out!

Birch Coulee Battlefield is near Morton. U.S. Army troops fought the Dakota there on September 2, 1862.

Grand Rapids' Forest History Center

C hat with the **lumberjacks.** They'll show you how they chop and saw. Next, climb aboard the wanigan. This floating shack drifts on the Mississippi River. You're touring an old-time logging camp! It's at the Forest History Center in Grand Rapids.

Minnesota's logging **industry** began in the 1830s. Lumberjacks cut down millions of pine trees. At first, oxen pulled the logs by chains. Later, horses pulled the logs on sleighs. The logs were floated down a river. Workers called river pigs rode atop the logs. They guided the logs along to sawmills. The logs were then sawed into lumber. It was used to build homes, schools, and barns.

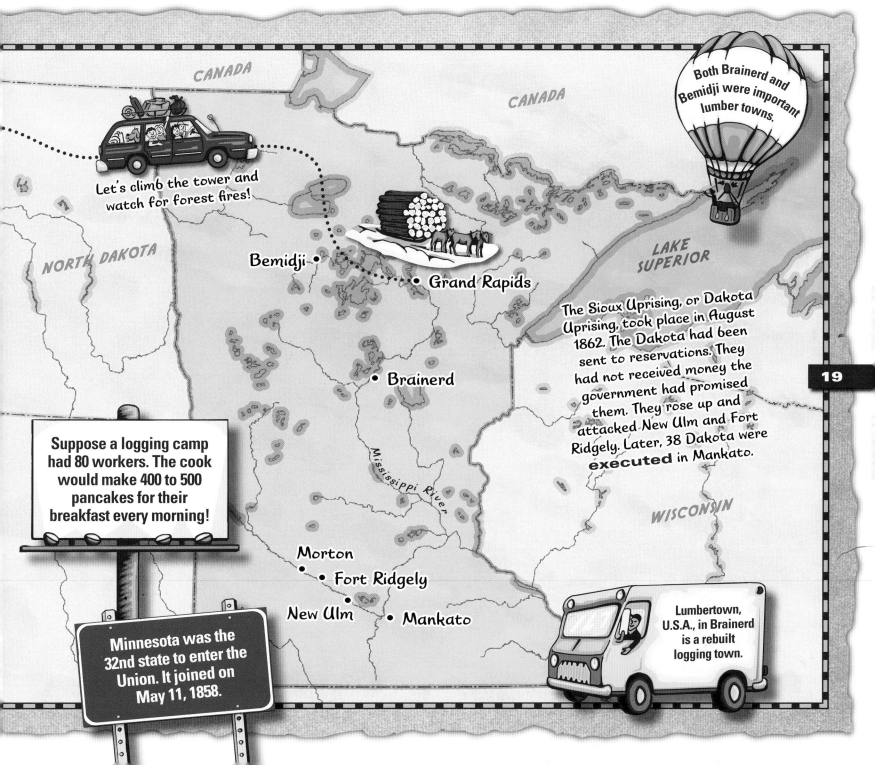

Both Brainerd and Bemidji were important lumber towns.

Let's climb the tower and watch for forest fires!

CANADA

CANADA

NORTH DAKOTA

LAKE SUPERIOR

Bemidji

Grand Rapids

The Sioux Uprising, or Dakota Uprising, took place in August 1862. The Dakota had been sent to reservations. They had not received money the government had promised them. They rose up and attacked New Ulm and Fort Ridgely. Later, 38 Dakota were **executed** in Mankato.

Brainerd

Mississippi River

WISCONSIN

Suppose a logging camp had 80 workers. The cook would make 400 to 500 pancakes for their breakfast every morning!

Morton

Fort Ridgely

New Ulm

Mankato

Minnesota was the 32nd state to enter the Union. It joined on May 11, 1858.

Lumbertown, U.S.A., in Brainerd is a rebuilt logging town.

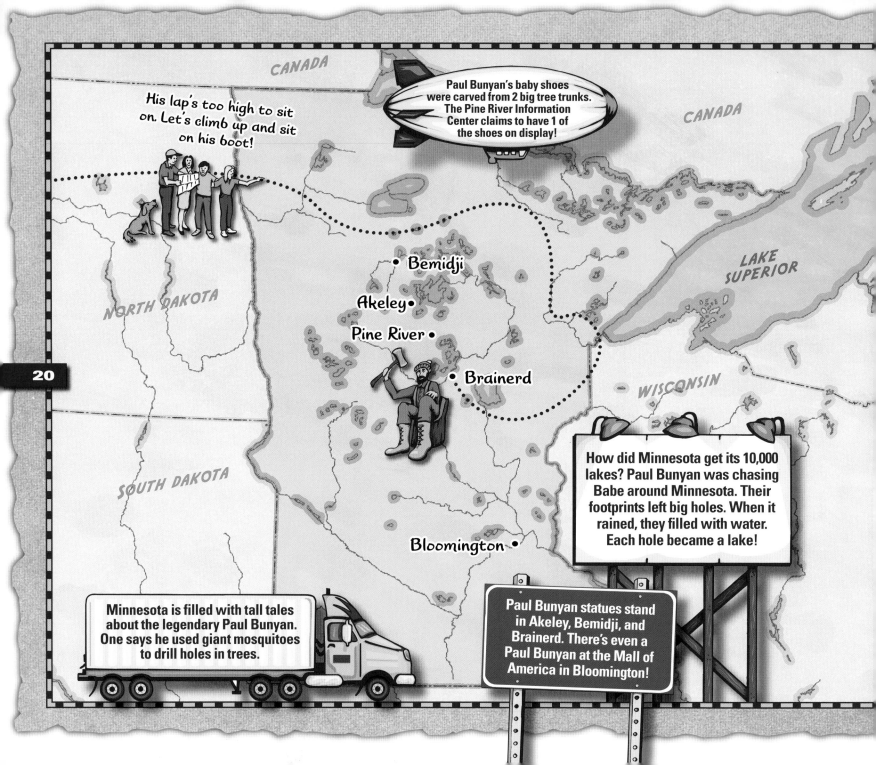

Paul Bunyan, the Giant Lumberjack

The big guy winks his eyes and talks. So maybe he's not so scary after all. But he's taller than a two-story building!

He's Paul Bunyan. You'll find him at Paul Bunyan Land. It's at This Old Farm in Brainerd. But what's this giant all about?

Lumberjacks had an imaginary hero. He was a giant lumberjack named Paul Bunyan. His sidekick was Babe the Blue Ox. Lumberjacks used to tell tall tales about their hero.

Giant Paul Bunyan statues stand in many cities today. You'll find them wherever lumberjacks lived!

Want to see a giant? Don't forget to visit Paul Bunyan in Brainerd!

Paul Bunyan's pet was Sport, the Reversible Dog. A logger accidentally cut Sport in half. He sewed Sport together with the front legs pointing down and the back legs pointing up.

The *William A. Irvin* Iron Ore Boat

Grab your life jacket! It's time to tour the *William A. Irvin!*

If you're in Duluth, head for the waterfront. There you'll climb aboard the *William A. Irvin.* It once carried iron **ore.** It sailed to ports along the Great Lakes. Sometimes it sailed through terrible storms.

Look down into the **cargo** area. It could hold thousands of tons of ore. Then visit the engine rooms. The engines are as big as cars!

Iron ore was first shipped from Minnesota in 1884. Minnesota soon became the leading iron-producing state. Thousands of **immigrants** came to northeastern Minnesota. The area's Mesabi Range was great for mining. It held massive deposits of iron ore.

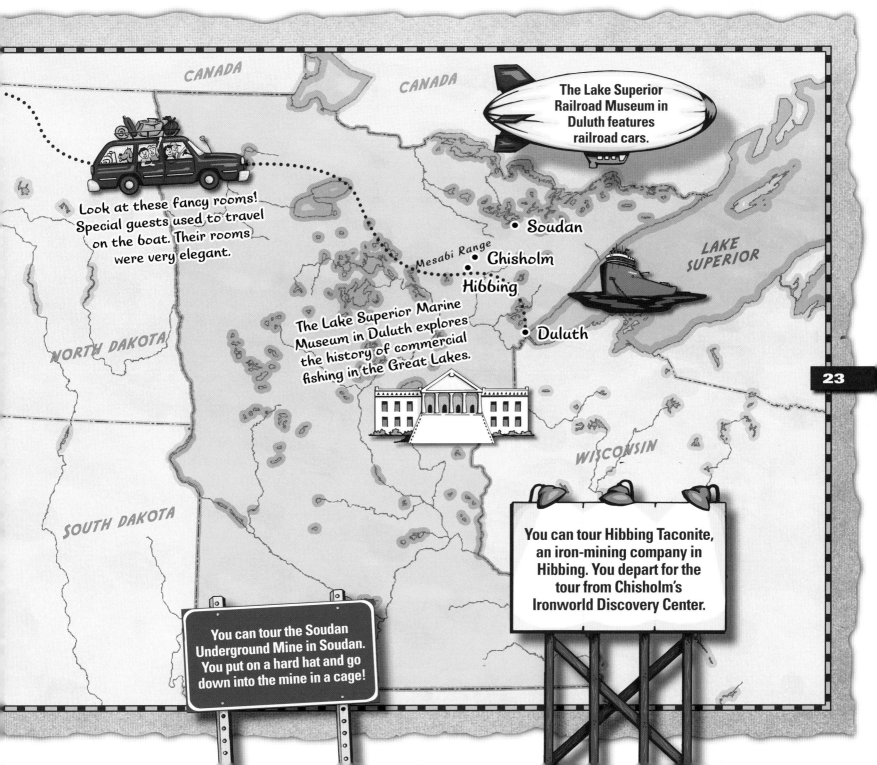

Look at these fancy rooms! Special guests used to travel on the boat. Their rooms were very elegant.

The Lake Superior Railroad Museum in Duluth features railroad cars.

• Soudan

Mesabi Range • Chisholm

Hibbing

• Duluth

The Lake Superior Marine Museum in Duluth explores the history of commercial fishing in the Great Lakes.

CANADA

CANADA

LAKE SUPERIOR

NORTH DAKOTA

SOUTH DAKOTA

WISCONSIN

You can tour the Soudan Underground Mine in Soudan. You put on a hard hat and go down into the mine in a cage!

You can tour Hibbing Taconite, an iron-mining company in Hibbing. You depart for the tour from Chisholm's Ironworld Discovery Center.

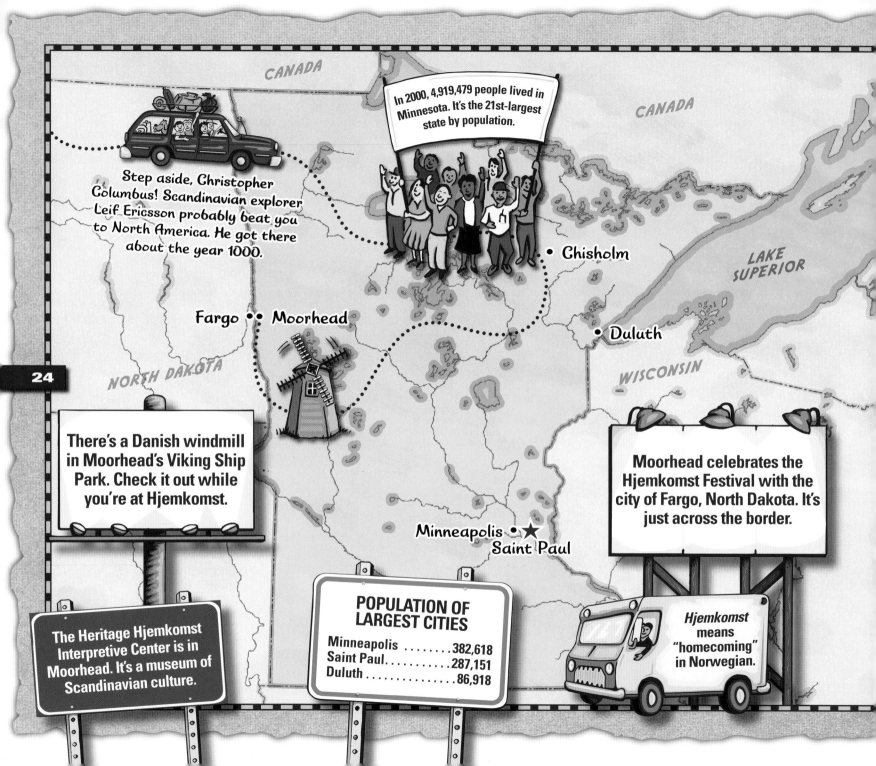

Step aside, Christopher Columbus! Scandinavian explorer Leif Ericsson probably beat you to North America. He got there about the year 1000.

In 2000, 4,919,479 people lived in Minnesota. It's the 21st-largest state by population.

CANADA

CANADA

LAKE SUPERIOR

Chisholm

Fargo • • Moorhead

Duluth

NORTH DAKOTA

WISCONSIN

There's a Danish windmill in Moorhead's Viking Ship Park. Check it out while you're at Hjemkomst.

Moorhead celebrates the Hjemkomst Festival with the city of Fargo, North Dakota. It's just across the border.

Minneapolis •★
Saint Paul

POPULATION OF LARGEST CITIES

Minneapolis 382,618
Saint Paul 287,151
Duluth 86,918

The Heritage Hjemkomst Interpretive Center is in Moorhead. It's a museum of Scandinavian culture.

Hjemkomst means "homecoming" in Norwegian.

Moorhead's Hjemkomst Festival

Ethnic Days in Chisholm celebrates the area's 8 ethnic groups.

See dancers in colorful folk costumes. Hear spooky tales about trolls. Try some *rommegrot*. It's a Norwegian cream mush. Then have some Swedish limpa bread. Finish up with some delicious *kringle*. That's a Danish pastry.

You're enjoying the Hjemkomst Festival! It celebrates Scandinavian **culture.** Scandinavians have roots in a group of countries. They are Norway, Sweden, Denmark, Finland, and Iceland.

Thousands of Scandinavians settled in Minnesota. Many were immigrants in the late 1800s. Their culture spread throughout the state. Scandinavians have a lot to celebrate!

This couple wears traditional Scandinavian dress. They're taking part in the Hjemkomst Festival.

In 2000, more than 3 out of 10 Minnesotans claimed Scandinavian roots.

New Ulm's Glockenspiel

Tick, tock. Tick, tock. Take time to visit the Glockenspiel in New Ulm.

New Ulm's Glockenspiel plays musical programs at 12:00 P.M., 3:00 P.M., and 5:00 P.M.

Clang, Clang, Clang! It's time for the Glockenspiel to play! That's the chiming clock tower in New Ulm. When it chimes, moving figures come out. They dance in a circle beneath the clock.

New Ulm is a very German town. German immigrants settled there in 1854.

Today, New Ulm still keeps many German **traditions.** Its festivals include Fasching and Oktoberfest. These festivals feature German music and food. People at Oktoberfest can even enjoy horse-drawn trolley rides through town.

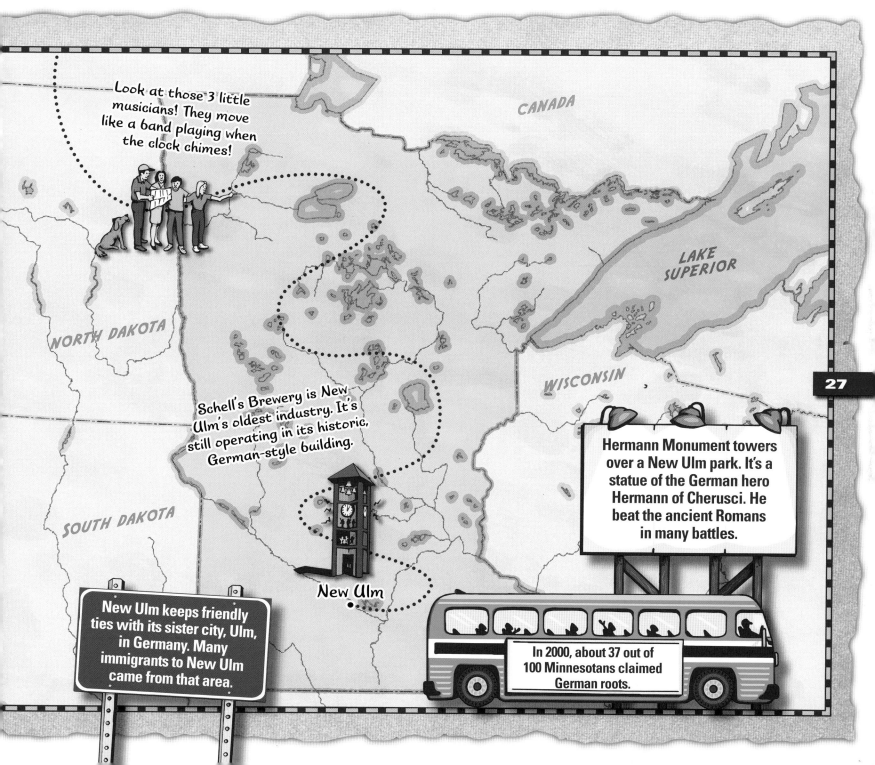

Look at those 3 little musicians! They move like a band playing when the clock chimes!

CANADA

LAKE SUPERIOR

NORTH DAKOTA

WISCONSIN

Schell's Brewery is New Ulm's oldest industry. It's still operating in its historic, German-style building.

Hermann Monument towers over a New Ulm park. It's a statue of the German hero Hermann of Cherusci. He beat the ancient Romans in many battles.

SOUTH DAKOTA

New Ulm

New Ulm keeps friendly ties with its sister city, Ulm, in Germany. Many immigrants to New Ulm came from that area.

In 2000, about 37 out of 100 Minnesotans claimed German roots.

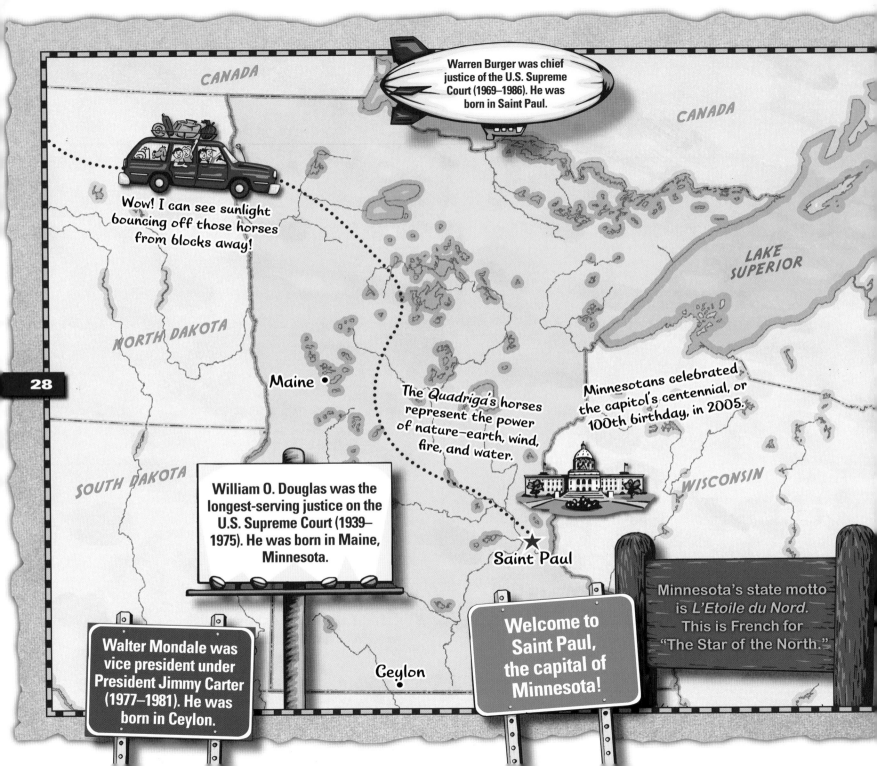

CANADA

CANADA

Warren Burger was chief justice of the U.S. Supreme Court (1969–1986). He was born in Saint Paul.

LAKE SUPERIOR

Wow! I can see sunlight bouncing off those horses from blocks away!

NORTH DAKOTA

Maine •

The Quadriga's horses represent the power of nature—earth, wind, fire, and water.

Minnesotans celebrated the capitol's centennial, or 100th birthday, in 2005.

SOUTH DAKOTA

WISCONSIN

William O. Douglas was the longest-serving justice on the U.S. Supreme Court (1939–1975). He was born in Maine, Minnesota.

★
Saint Paul

Minnesota's state motto is *L'Etoile du Nord.* This is French for "The Star of the North."

Walter Mondale was vice president under President Jimmy Carter (1977–1981). He was born in Ceylon.

Ceylon •

Welcome to Saint Paul, the capital of Minnesota!

The State Capitol in Saint Paul

Minnesota's capitol is gleaming white. But something gold flashes out above the entrance. It's a huge sculpture called the *Quadriga*. It shows four golden horses pulling a golden carriage. You can get right up close to them, too. Just take a capitol tour!

The capitol houses many important state government offices. For example, the state legislature meets there. It's one of Minnesota's three branches of government. Its members make the state's laws. Another branch of government carries out the laws. This branch is led by the governor. The third branch consists of judges. They decide whether laws have been broken.

The *Quadriga* shines atop the entrance to Minnesota's capitol.

Hubert Humphrey was vice president under President Lyndon Johnson (1965–1969). He was born in South Dakota but lived in Minnesota as an adult.

Minneapolis's Cherry in a Spoon

Are cherries your favorite fruit? Then you'll love touring Minneapolis's Sculpture Garden!

Minneapolis and Saint Paul are called the Twin Cities.

Do you like cherries? How about a cherry bigger than you? You'll see one in Minneapolis's Sculpture Garden. It's a giant cherry in a giant spoon. And water spews out the cherry's stem!

There are many amazing sights in Minneapolis. Just take a walk along the riverfront. You'll see the huge Stone Arch Bridge. Then hop aboard a riverboat. You'll view the city from the Mississippi River. If you like shopping, stroll along Nicollet Mall. It's twelve blocks long!

To relax, head for one of Minneapolis's parks. You can ride a bike for miles. Or just lounge by a lake. There's something for everyone in Minneapolis!

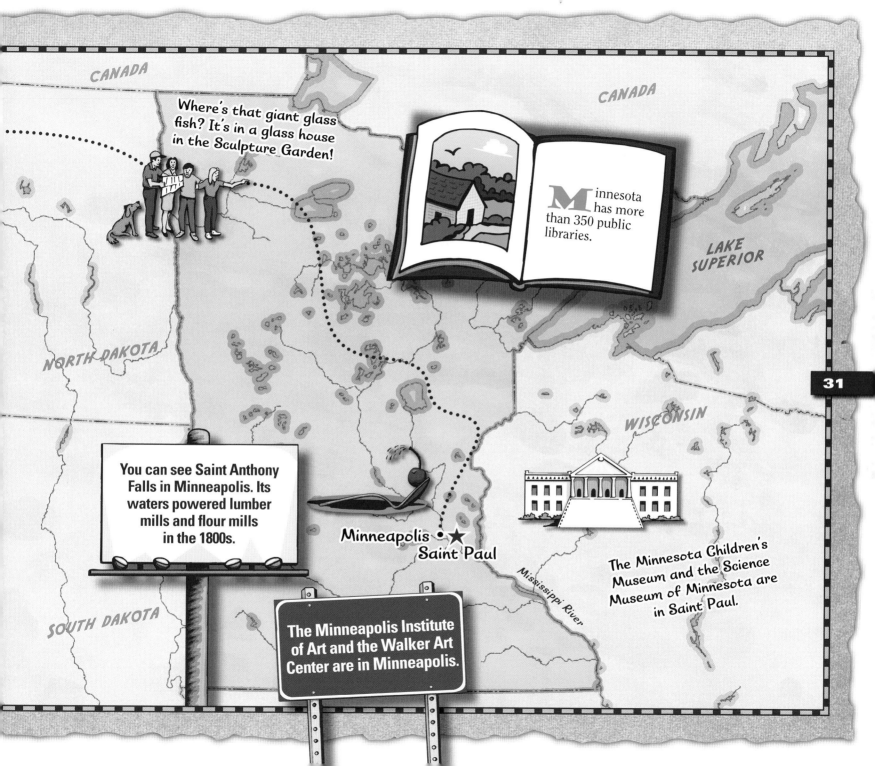

Where's that giant glass fish? It's in a glass house in the Sculpture Garden!

Minnesota has more than 350 public libraries.

You can see Saint Anthony Falls in Minneapolis. Its waters powered lumber mills and flour mills in the 1800s.

Minneapolis • ★
Saint Paul

The Minneapolis Institute of Art and the Walker Art Center are in Minneapolis.

The Minnesota Children's Museum and the Science Museum of Minnesota are in Saint Paul.

CANADA

CANADA

LAKE SUPERIOR

NORTH DAKOTA

WISCONSIN

SOUTH DAKOTA

Mississippi River

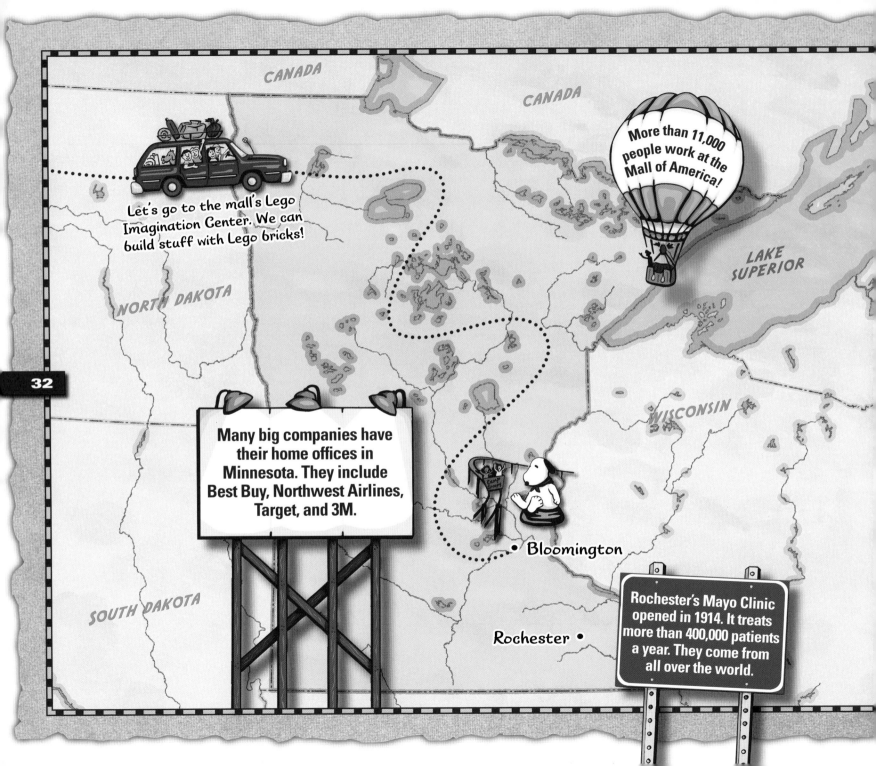

Let's go to the mall's Lego Imagination Center. We can build stuff with Lego bricks!

More than 11,000 people work at the Mall of America!

Many big companies have their home offices in Minnesota. They include Best Buy, Northwest Airlines, Target, and 3M.

Rochester's Mayo Clinic opened in 1914. It treats more than 400,000 patients a year. They come from all over the world.

CANADA

CANADA

LAKE SUPERIOR

NORTH DAKOTA

WISCONSIN

SOUTH DAKOTA

Bloomington

Rochester

Shop Till You Drop in Bloomington

Do you like hanging out at the mall? Then check out the Mall of America. It's in Bloomington, just outside of Minneapolis. It's the nation's largest mall under one roof!

This mall has more than 400 stores. But that's not all. It has a theme park called Camp Snoopy. It also has an aquarium with sharks. People come here from all over the world!

In the 1900s, Minnesota changed in many ways. Its service industries grew fast. Those are businesses that offer services, not goods. They include stores such as those in the mall. Many banks and hospitals opened, too. Rochester's Mayo Clinic became world famous.

Want a break from shopping? Head to the aquarium in the Mall of America.

The Mayo Clinic has a medical library in Rochester with more than 350,000 books.

Spam was first produced in 1937.

Young visitors wear special gear at Austin's Spam Museum.

More than 6 billion cans of Spam had been sold as of 2002!

Austin's Spam Museum

Do you like Spam? Not the computer kind. This Spam is a famous canned lunch meat. Just visit the Spam Museum!

First you see the towering Wall of Spam. It's made of thousands of Spam cans. Then you can watch videos about Spam. You can take the Spam Exam. Or try getting some Spam into a can!

Meat processing is a big industry in Minnesota. Cattle, hogs, turkeys, and chickens provide the meat. It goes to meat plants. There it's ground up and cooked. Finally, it's packaged for stores.

Minnesota factories make many other products. But only Spam has its own museum!

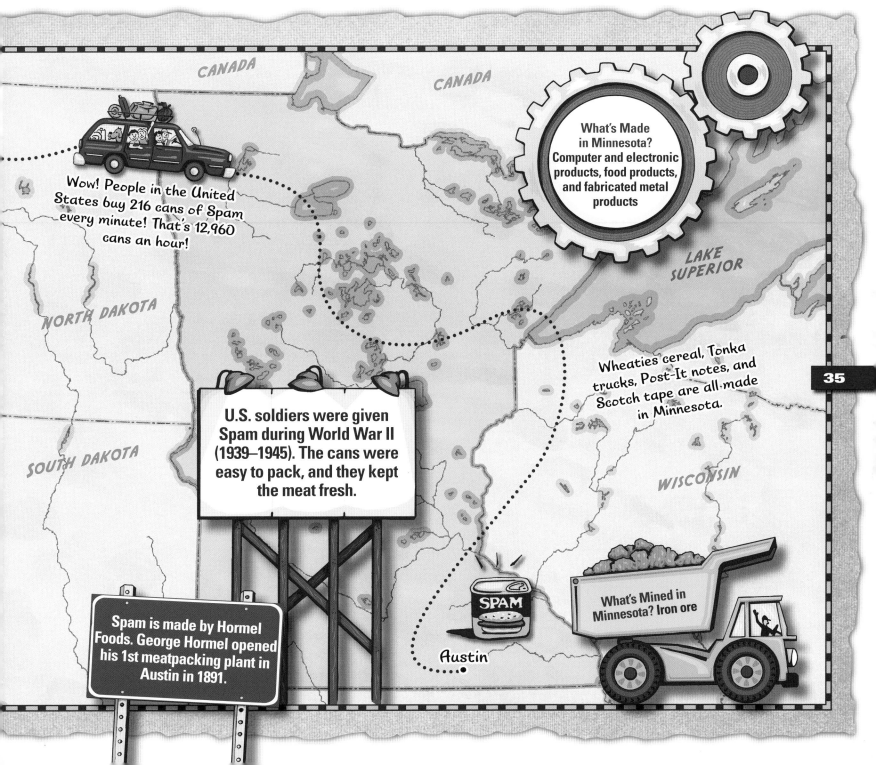

Wow! People in the United States buy 216 cans of Spam every minute! That's 12,960 cans an hour!

What's Made in Minnesota? Computer and electronic products, food products, and fabricated metal products

Wheaties cereal, Tonka trucks, Post-It notes, and Scotch tape are all made in Minnesota.

U.S. soldiers were given Spam during World War II (1939–1945). The cans were easy to pack, and they kept the meat fresh.

Spam is made by Hormel Foods. George Hormel opened his 1st meatpacking plant in Austin in 1891.

What's Mined in Minnesota? Iron ore

Austin

CANADA
CANADA
NORTH DAKOTA
SOUTH DAKOTA
LAKE SUPERIOR
WISCONSIN

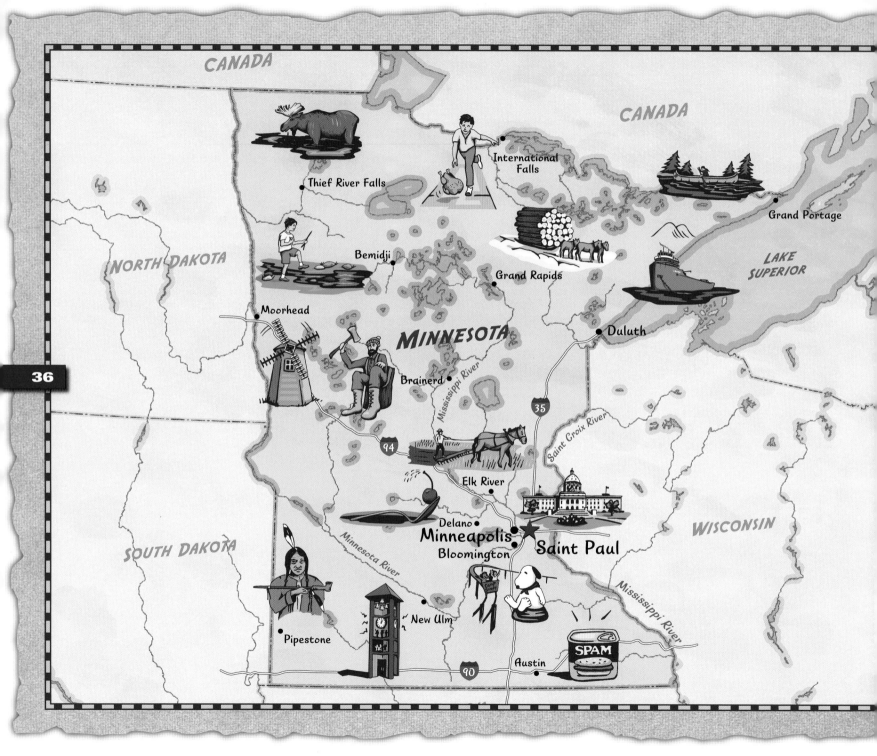

CANADA

CANADA

Thief River Falls

International Falls

Grand Portage

NORTH DAKOTA

Bemidji

LAKE SUPERIOR

Grand Rapids

Moorhead

Duluth

MINNESOTA

Brainerd

Mississippi River

35

Saint Croix River

94

Elk River

Delano

Minneapolis

Saint Paul

WISCONSIN

Bloomington

SOUTH DAKOTA

Minnesota River

Pipestone

New Ulm

Mississippi River

Austin

90

SPAM

OUR TRIP

We visited many amazing places on our trip! We also met a lot of interesting people along the way. Look at the map on the left. Use your finger to trace all the places we have been.

What real town is Frostbite Falls based on? See page 10 for the answer.

Which Minnesota towns feature Paul Bunyan statues? Page 20 has the answer.

When did Leif Ericsson arrive in North America? See page 24 for the answer.

How many Minnesotans claim Scandinavian roots? Look on page 25 for the answer.

Who was the longest-serving justice on the U.S. Supreme Court? Page 28 has the answer.

Which 2 cities are called the Twin Cities? Turn to page 30 for the answer.

How many public libraries does Minnesota have? Look on page 31 for the answer.

How many cans of Spam are sold each minute? Turn to page 35 for the answer.

That was a great trip! We have traveled all over Minnesota!
There are a few places we didn't have time for, though. Next time, we plan to visit Apple Jack Orchards in Delano. Visitors can pick raspberries, strawberries, and apples. In winter, people can even buy a Christmas tree there!

More Places to Visit in Minnesota

WORDS TO KNOW

cargo (KAR-goh) goods that are transported in large amounts on some kind of vehicle

culture (KUHL-chur) a group of people's customs, beliefs, and way of life

executed (EK-suh-kyoot-uhd) killed as a punishment for a crime

immigrants (IM-uh-gruhnts) people who leave their home country and move to another country

industry (IN-duh-stree) a type of business

lumberjacks (LUHM-bur-jaks) workers in the logging business who cut down trees and transport logs

ore (OR) rock that contains valuable metals such as iron or gold

rendezvous (RON-day-voo) French word for a meeting

reservation (rez-ur-VAY-shuhn) land set aside for special use, such as for Native Americans

traditions (truh-DISH-unz) long-held customs

voyageurs (voy-uh-ZHURZ) people working for fur companies who traveled between the wilderness and trading posts

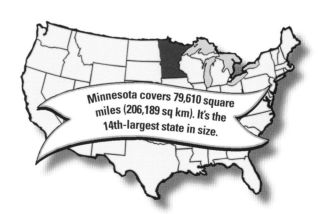

Minnesota covers 79,610 square miles (206,189 sq km). It's the 14th-largest state in size.

STATE SYMBOLS

State bird: Common loon

State butterfly: Monarch butterfly

State drink: Milk

State fish: Walleye

State flower: Pink and white lady's slipper

State gemstone: Lake Superior agate

State grain: Wild rice

State muffin: Blueberry muffin

State mushroom: Morel

State tree: Red pine

State flag

State seal

STATE SONG

"Hail! Minnesota"

Words by Truman E. Rickard and Arthur E. Upson,

music by Truman E. Rickard

Minnesota, hail to thee!
Hail to thee, our state so dear!
Thy light shall ever be
A beacon bright and clear.
Thy sons and daughters true
Will proclaim thee near and far,
They shall guard thy fame
And adore thy name;
Thou shalt be their Northern Star.

Like the stream that bends to sea,
Like the pine that seeks the blue,
Minnesota, still for thee
Thy sons are strong and true.
From the woods and waters fair;
From the prairies waving far,
At thy call they throng
With their shout and song,
Hailing thee their Northern Star.

FAMOUS PEOPLE

Bender, Chief (1884–1954), baseball player

Berg, Patty (1918–), golfer

Coen, Ethan (1957–), Joel (1954–), filmmakers

DiCamillo, Kate (1964–), children's author

Dylan, Bob (1941–), musician and songwriter

Fitzgerald, F. Scott (1896–1940), author

Garland, Judy (1922–1969), actor and singer

Keillor, Garrison (1942–), radio host and writer

Lewis, Sinclair (1885–1951), novelist

Lovelace, Maud Hart (1892–1980), children's author

Madden, John (1936–), football coach and broadcaster

Maris, Roger (1934–1985), baseball player

Mayo, William Worrall (1819–1911), doctor who founded the Mayo Clinic

Mondale, Walter (1928–), politician

Nagurski, Bronko (1908–1990), football player

O'Brien, Tim (1946–), author

Prince (1958–), musician and songwriter

Ryder, Winona (1971–), actor

Schulz, Charles M. (1922–2000), creator of the comic strip *Peanuts*

Ventura, Jesse (1951–), wrestler and former governor of Minnesota

Wilkins, Roy (1901–1981), civil rights leader

TO FIND OUT MORE

At the Library
Bowen, Betsy. *Gathering: A Northwoods Counting Book.* Boston: Houghton Mifflin, 1999.

Keillor, Garrison, Steve Johnson (illustrator), and Lou Fancher (illustrator). *Cat, You Better Come Home.* New York: Viking, 1995.

Klingel, Cynthia Fitterer, and Robert B. Noyed. *Charles Schulz.* Chanhassen, Minn.: The Child's World, 2002.

Lovelace, Maud Hart, and Lois Lenski (illustrator). *Betsy-Tacy.* New York: Harper Trophy, 2000.

Wargin, Kathy-Jo, Karen Latham (illustrator), and Rebecca Latham (illustrator). *V Is for Viking: A Minnesota Alphabet.* Chelsea, Mich.: Sleeping Bear Press, 2003.

On the Web
Visit our home page for lots of links about Minnesota: *http://www.childsworld.com/links*

Note to Parents, Teachers, and Librarians: We routinely verify our Web links to make sure they are safe, active sites—so encourage your readers to check them out!

Places to Visit or Contact
Explore Minnesota Tourism
121 7th Place E
Metro Square, Suite 100
Saint Paul, MN 55101
800/657-3700
For more information about traveling in Minnesota

Minnesota Historical Society
345 West Kellogg Boulevard
Saint Paul, MN 55102
651/296-6126
For more information about the history of Minnesota

INDEX

Bye, North Star State.
We had a great time.
We'll come back soon!